HOLIDAY PATTERNS

Compiled by Jean Warren

Illustrated by Gary Mohrmann

Warren Publishing House, Inc.
Everett, Washington

Special thanks to Judy Coskey for her help with the Hanukkah patterns.

Editorial Staff:

  Gayle Bittinger, Kathleen Cubley, Jean Warren

Production Staff:

  Manager: Eileen Carbary; *Assistant:* Jo Anna Brock

  Book and Cover Design: Kathy Kotomaimoce

  Computer Graphics: Carol DeBolt, Eric Stovall

ISBN: 0-911019-45-6

Printed in the United States of America
Published by: Warren Publishing House, Inc.
        P.O. Box 2250
        Everett, WA 98203

CONTENTS

Using Holiday Patterns

Mix and match the patterns in this book to create a variety of teaching props, learning games, bulletin boards and more. Following are some suggestions of ways to use the patterns. Adapt these ideas or make up your own — the only limit is your imagination.

Language

Stick Puppets — Color and cut out photocopies of the smallest holiday shapes and glue them to craft sticks or tongue depressors.

Stand-Up Story Characters— Use the patterns as guides to cut various sizes and kinds of holiday shapes out of posterboard. Make stands for the shapes out of posterboard or playdough.

Magnetic Story Characters — Use the patterns as guides to cut holiday shapes out of construction paper or posterboard and attach magnets to the backs of them.

Flannelboard Story Characters — Use the patterns as guides to cut holiday shapes out of felt or construction paper backed with felt strips.

Picture Books — Photocopy holiday shapes of the same size, arrange them in the desired order and staple them together to make books. Add construction paper covers, if desired.

Draw-A-Story — Cut out several photocopied shapes, cover them with clear self-stick paper and put them in a bag or a box. Let the children take turns pulling out a shape for you to incorporate into a story.

Music And Movement

Finger Puppets — Color and cut out photocopies of the smallest holiday shapes and attach them to construction paper or pipe cleaner "rings." Use the finger puppets while reciting poems or singing holiday songs.

Holiday Songs — Use the patterns as guides to cut holiday shapes out of construction paper or felt. Use the shapes as props while singing songs or telling stories.

Art

Stencils — Use the patterns as guides to cut holiday shapes out of large pieces of posterboard or tag board to make stencils.

Stamps — Use the patterns as guides to cut holiday shapes out of sponges. Glue the sponge shapes on blocks of wood to make stamps.

Necklaces — Use the smaller patterns as guides to cut holiday shapes out of construction paper. Let the children each decorate one or more shapes. Have the children string their shapes on pieces of yarn.

Classroom Aids

Room Decorations — Use the patterns as guides to cut out holiday shapes for decorating bulletin boards or creating a frieze.

Name Tags — Use the patterns as guides to cut holiday shapes out of construction paper. Write a child's name on each shape and string it on a piece of yarn.

Calendar Markers — Use one of the smaller patterns as a guide to cut holiday shapes, one for each day of the month, out of construction paper. Number the shapes and arrange them in a calendar format on a bulletin board.

Learning Games

Matching — Use the patterns as guides to cut various sizes and kinds of holiday shapes out of various colors of construction paper or felt. Let the children match the shapes by size, kind or color.

Counting — Use the patterns as guides to cut various sizes and kinds of holiday shapes out of various colors of construction paper or felt. Ask the children to count all of the red shapes or all of the car shapes.

Sizing — Use the patterns as guides to cut four sizes of one object's shape out of construction paper or felt. Have the children arrange the shapes by size.

Sorting — Use the patterns as guides to cut various sizes and kinds of holiday shapes out of various colors of construction paper or felt. Let the children sort the shapes by size, kind, color or type.

Card Games — Photocopy and cut out the game cards. Cover them with clear self-stick paper. Help the children use the cards to play such games as *Go Fish, Concentration, Lotto* and *Bingo*.

Bat 9

Cat 11

Cat 13

Cornstalk 15

Ghost 19

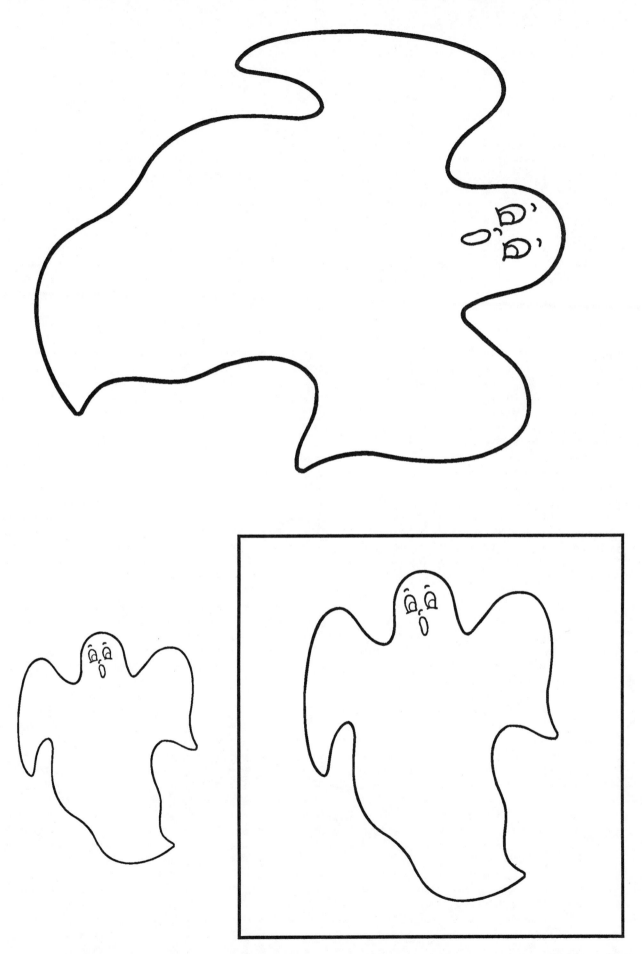

Ghost 21

Jack-O'-Lantern 25

Scarecrow 27

Scarecrow 29

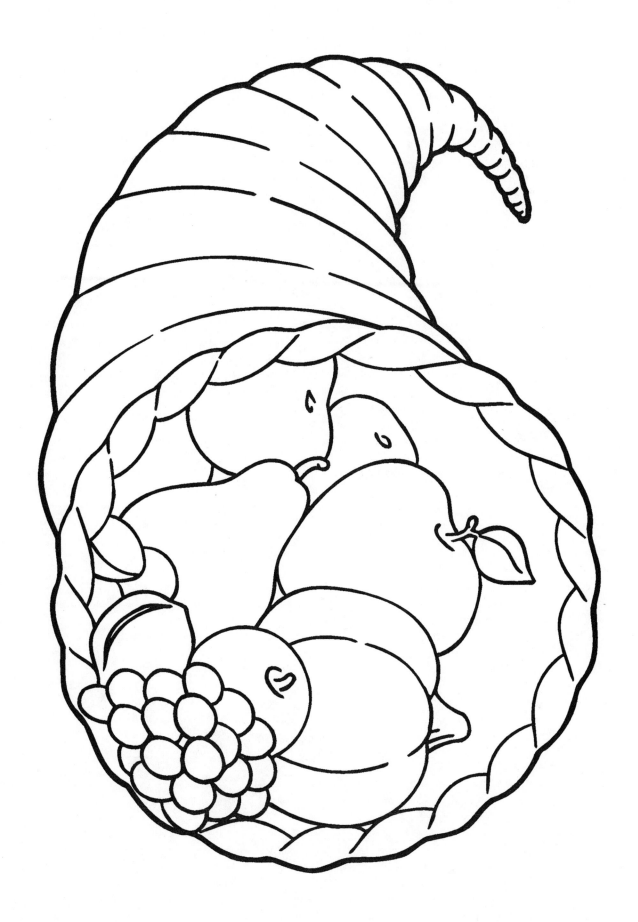

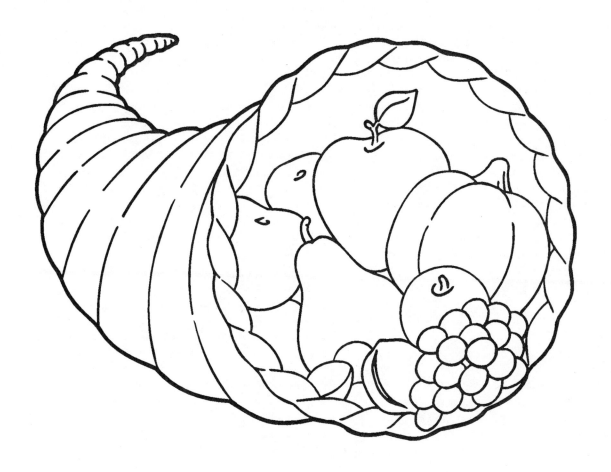

Cornucopia

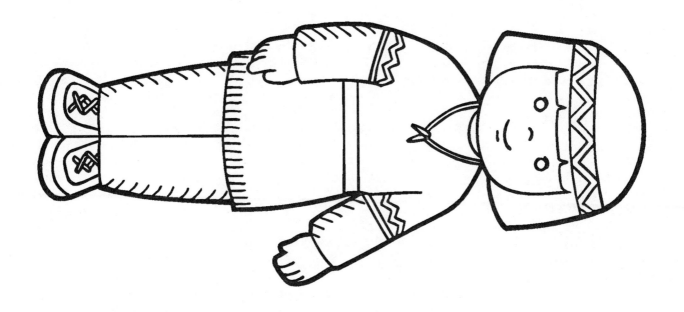

Native American 37

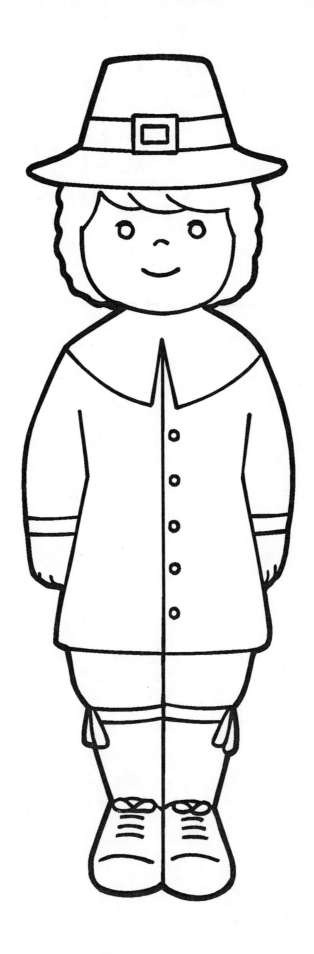

Pilgrim Boy 39

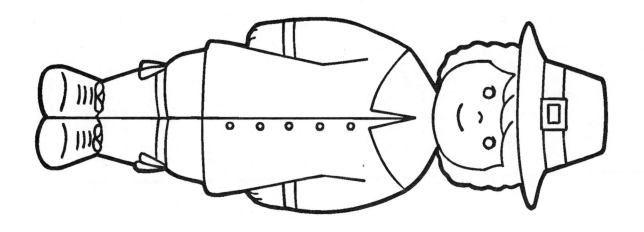

Pilgrim Boy 41

Pilgrim Girl 43

Pilgrim Girl 45

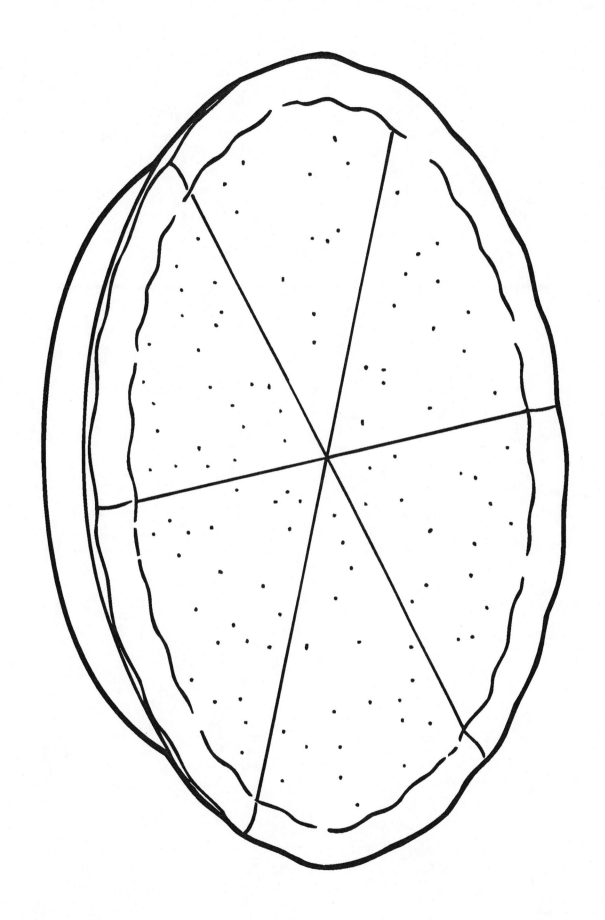

Pumpkin Pie 47

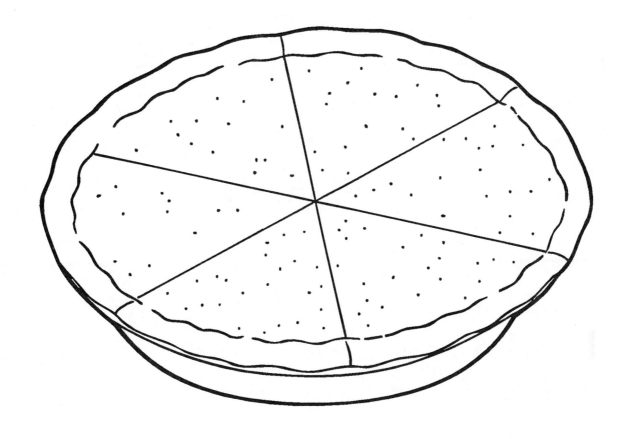

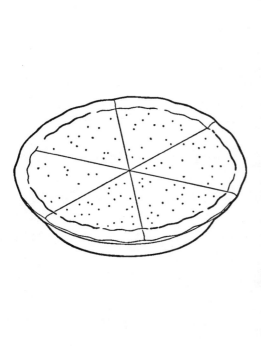

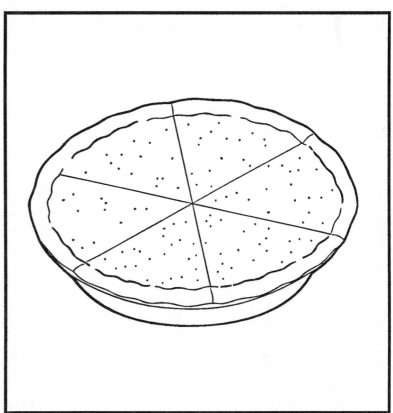

Pumpkin Pie   49

Turkey 51

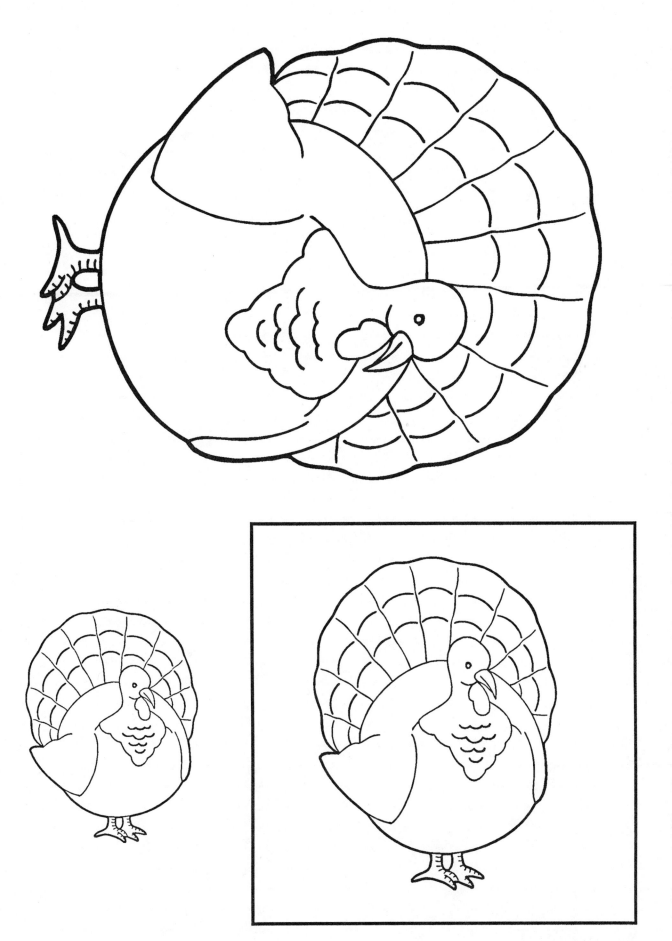

Turkey 53

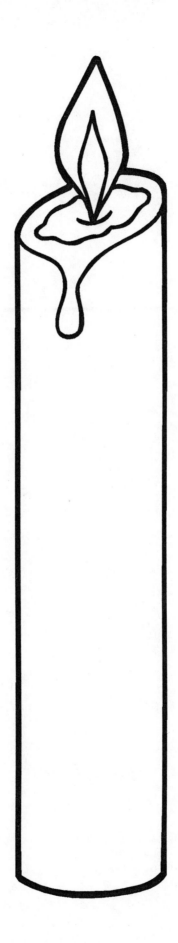

Candle 55

Candle 57

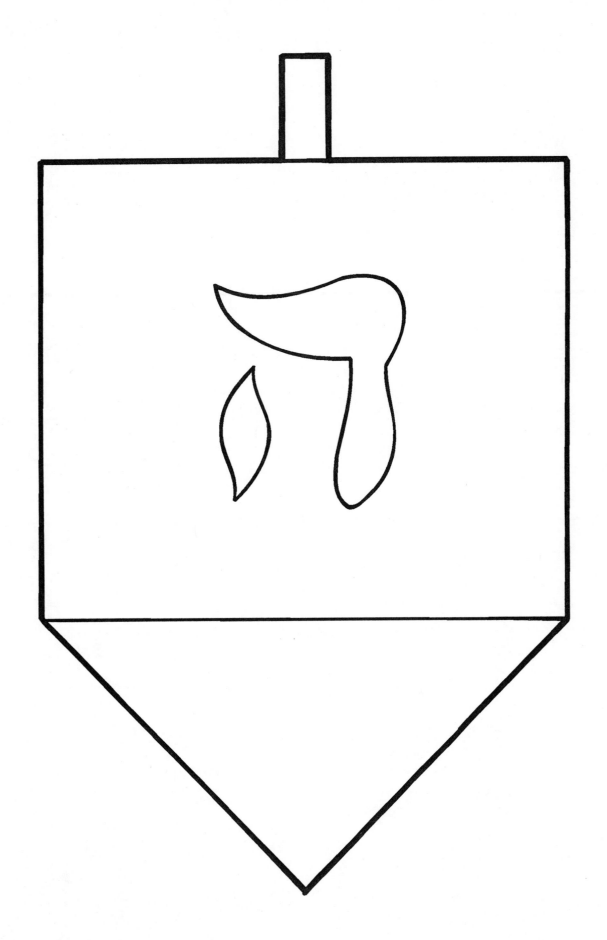

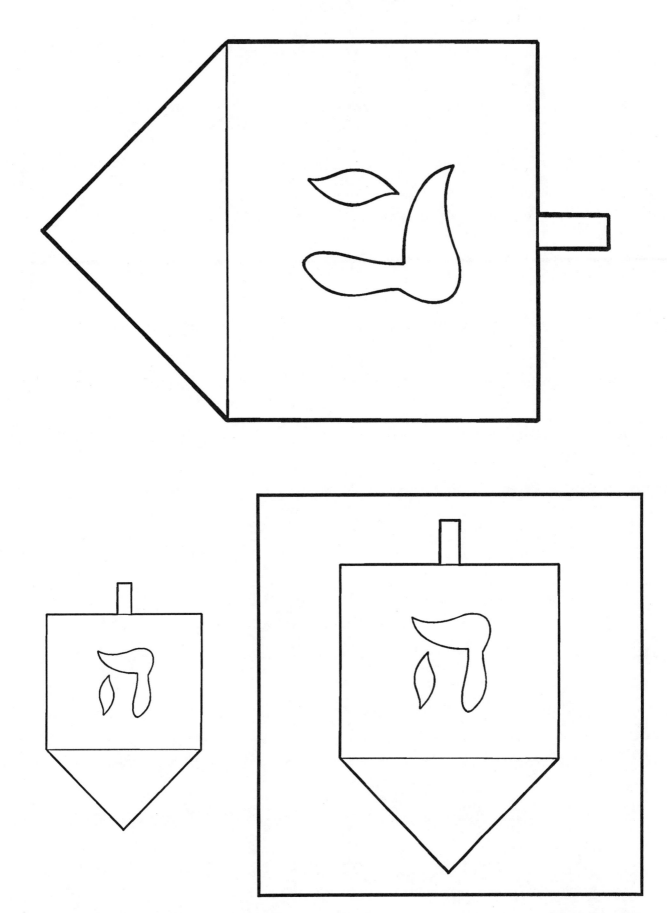

Dreidle 61

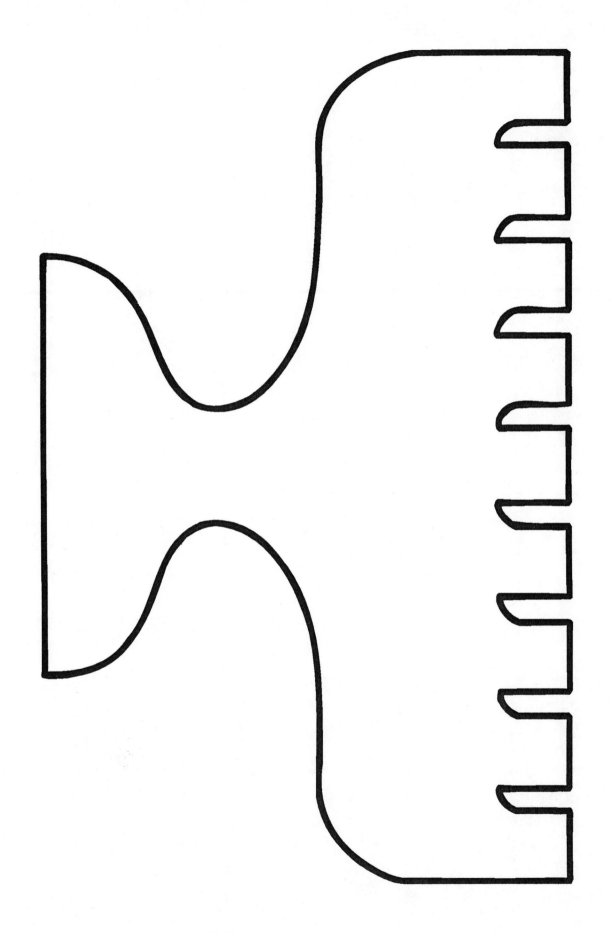

Menorah 63

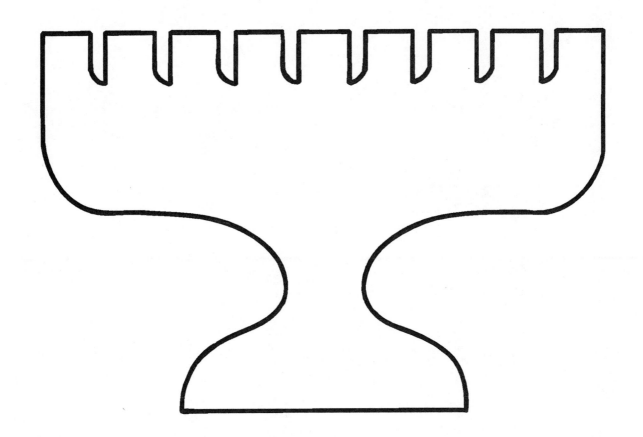

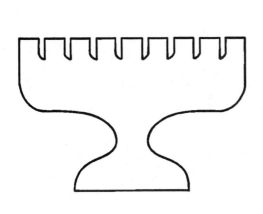

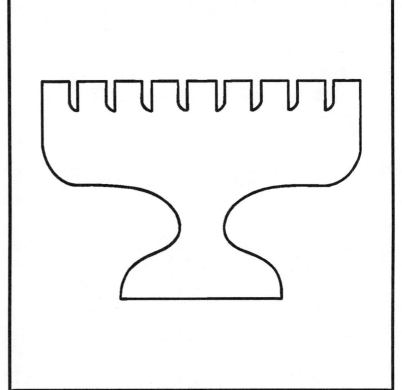

Menorah 65

Star Of David 67

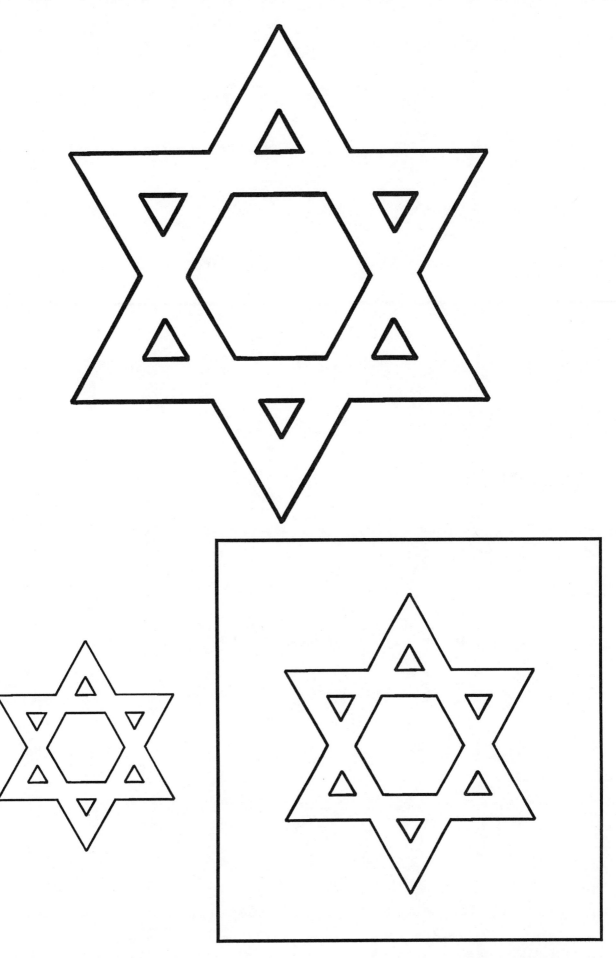

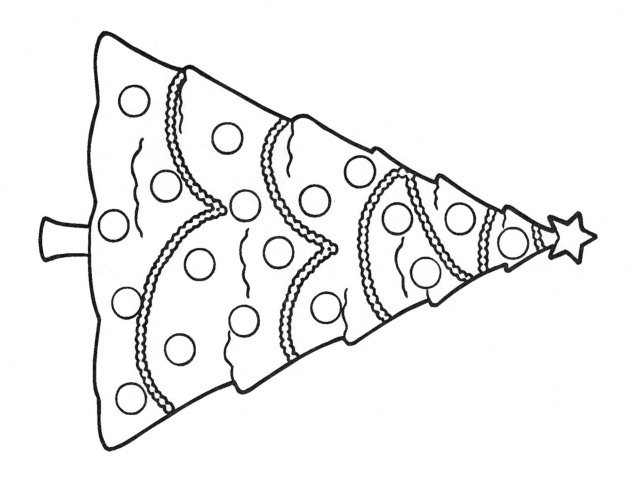

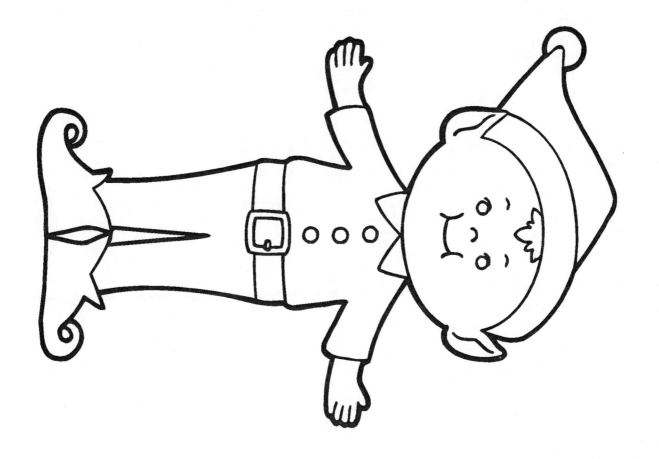

Elf 77

Gingerbread Cookie 79

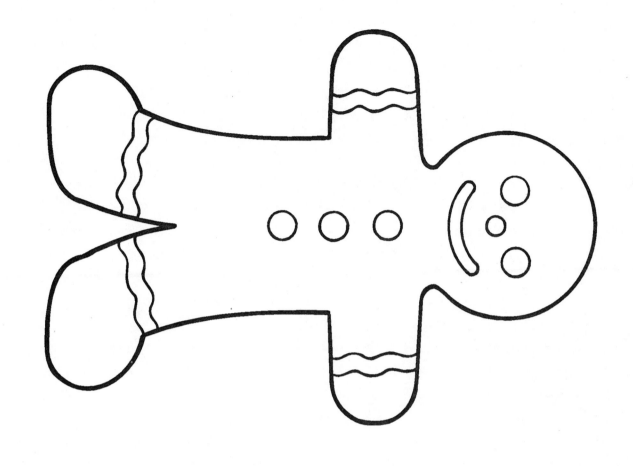

Gingerbread Cookie 81

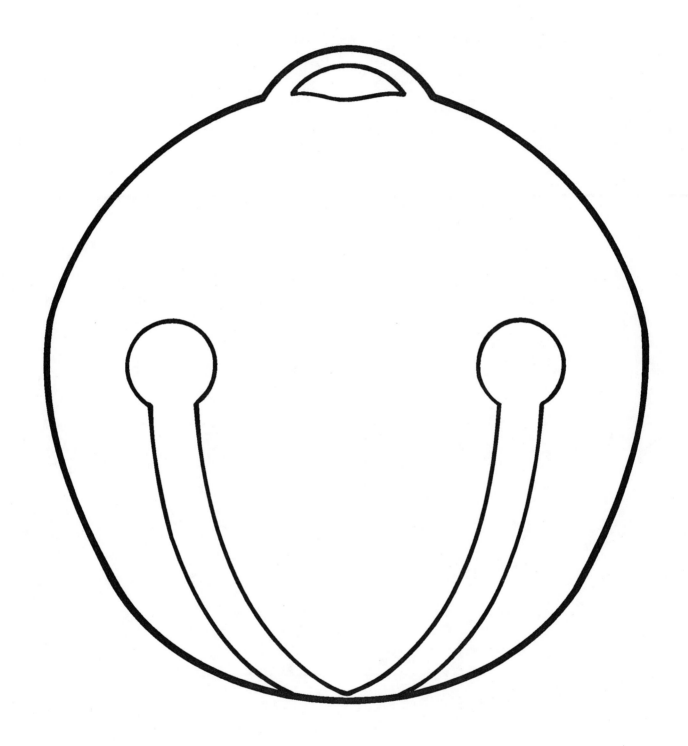

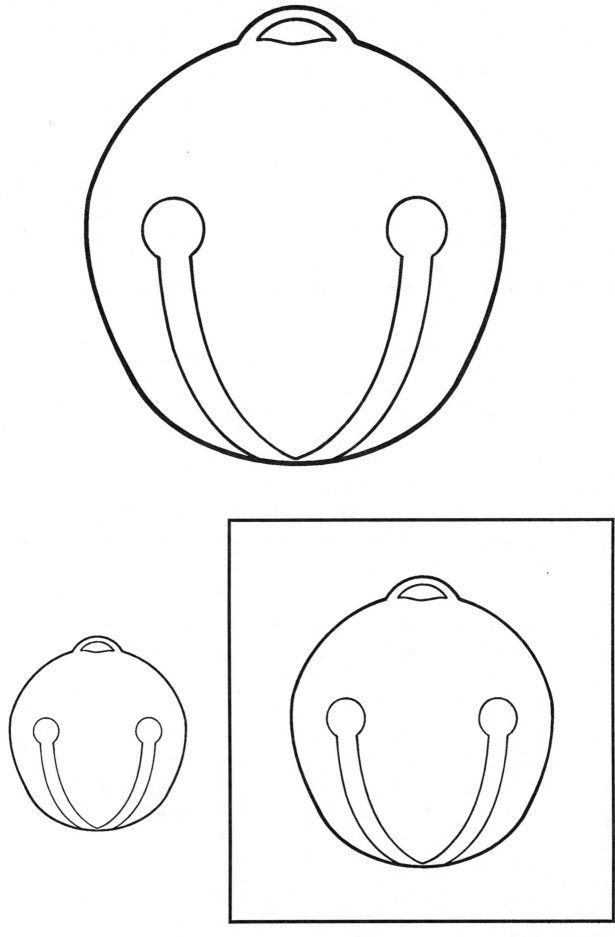

Jingle Bell 85

Poinsettia 87

Poinsettia 89

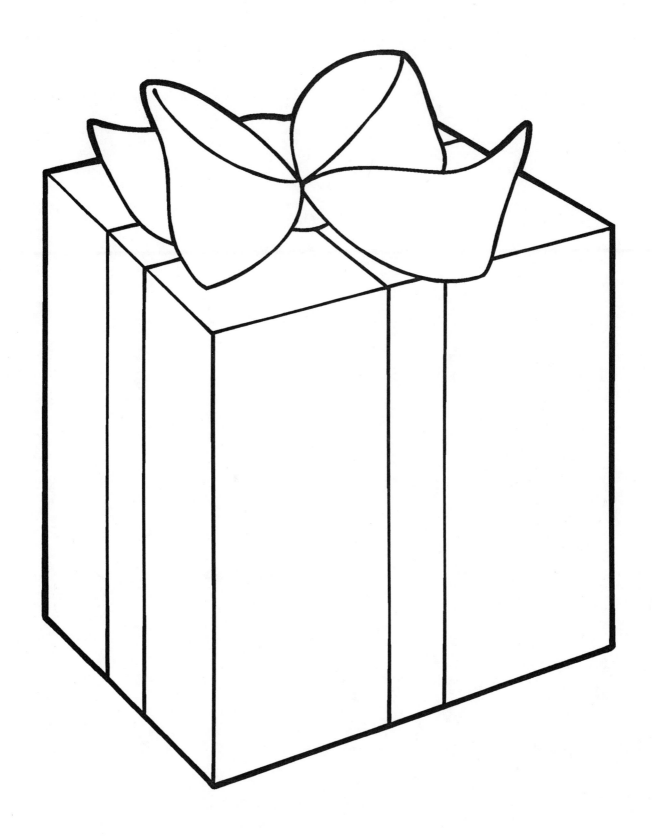

Present 91

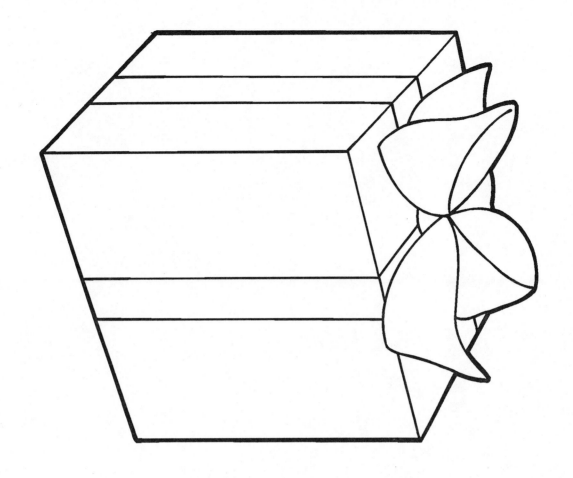

Reindeer 97

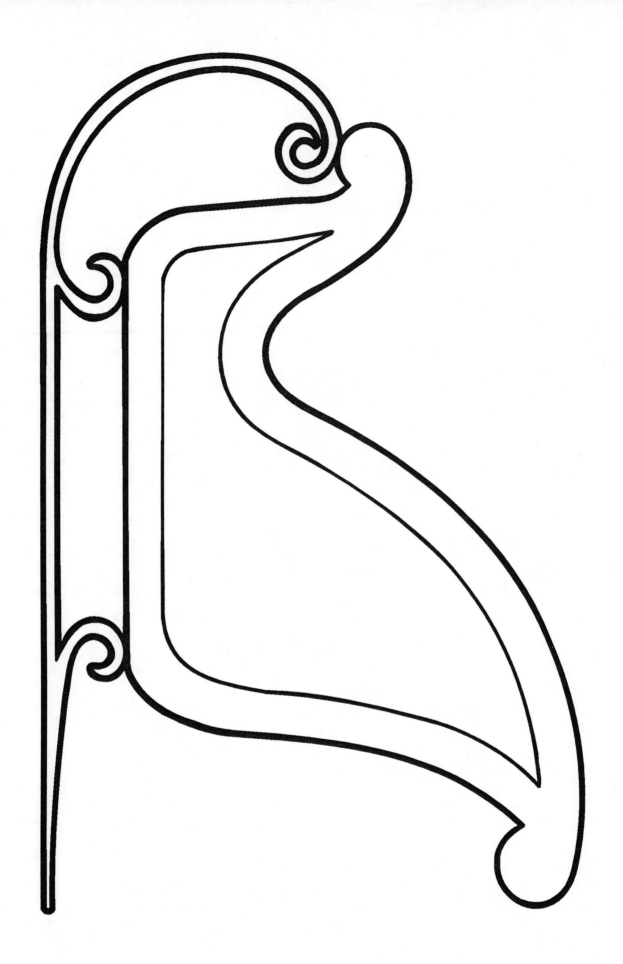

Sleigh   103

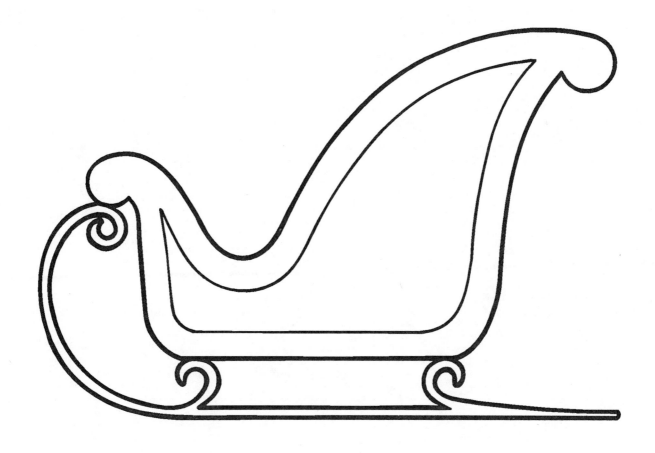

Star   107

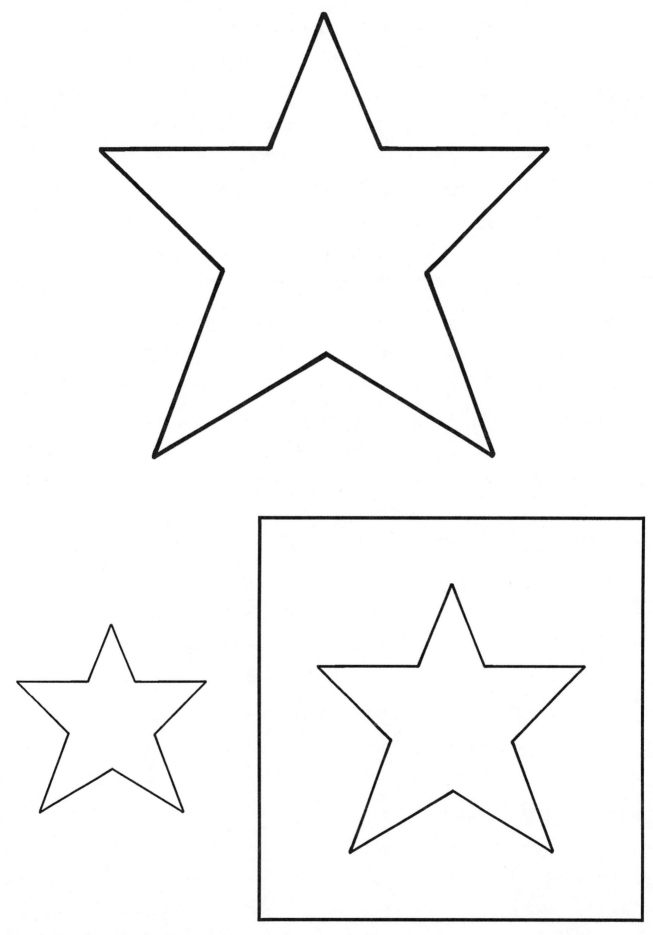

Star 109

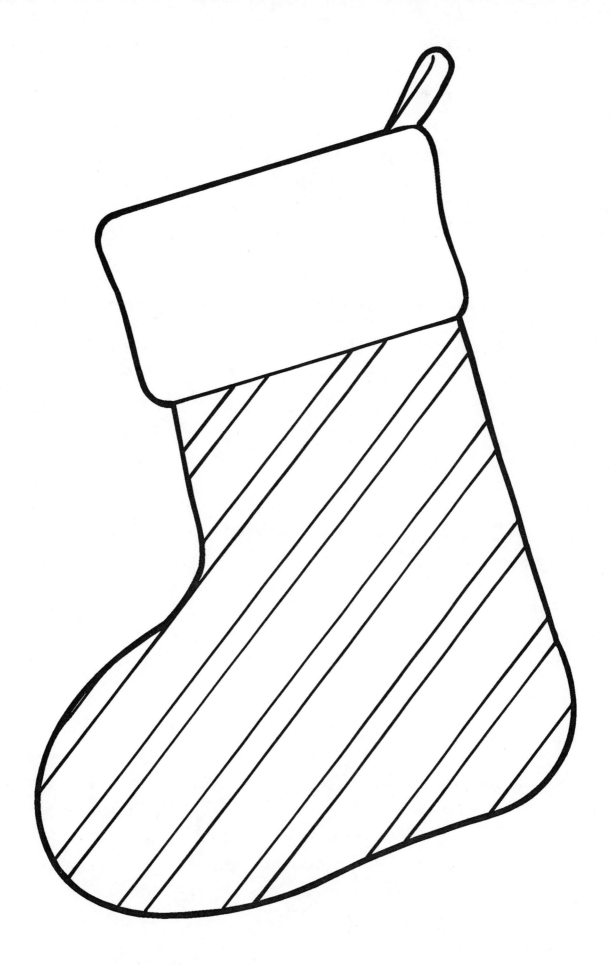

Stocking 111

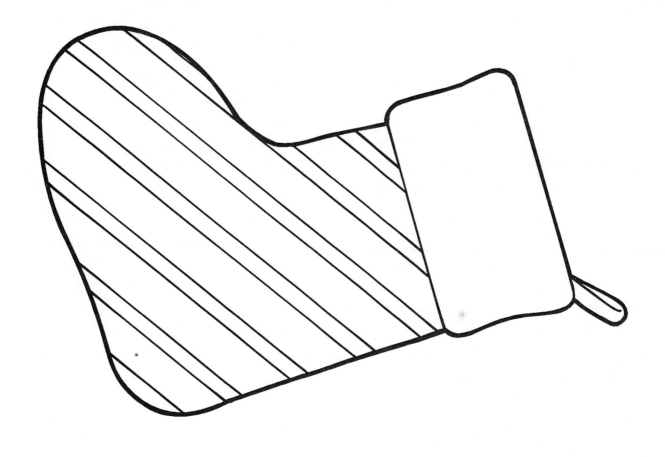

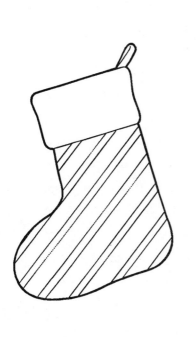

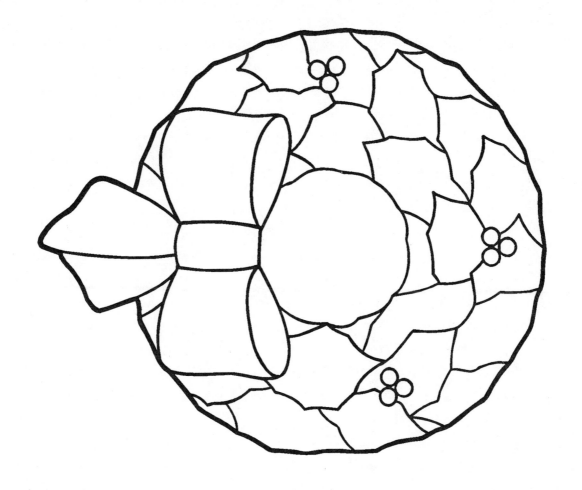

Wreath 117

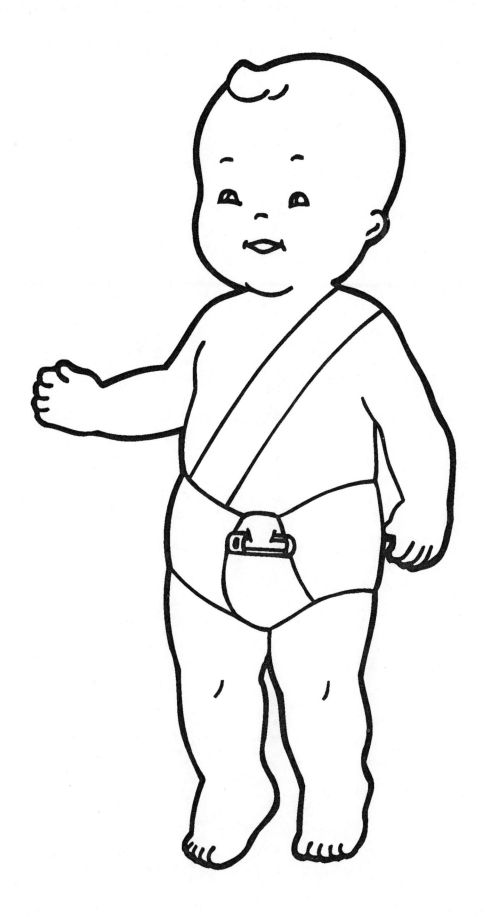

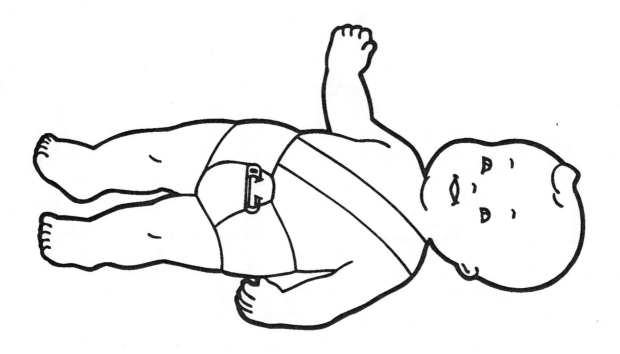

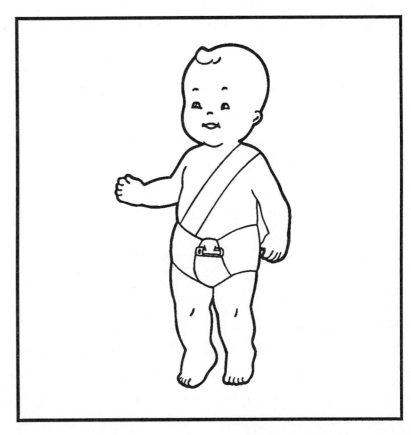

Party Hat 123

Party Hat 125

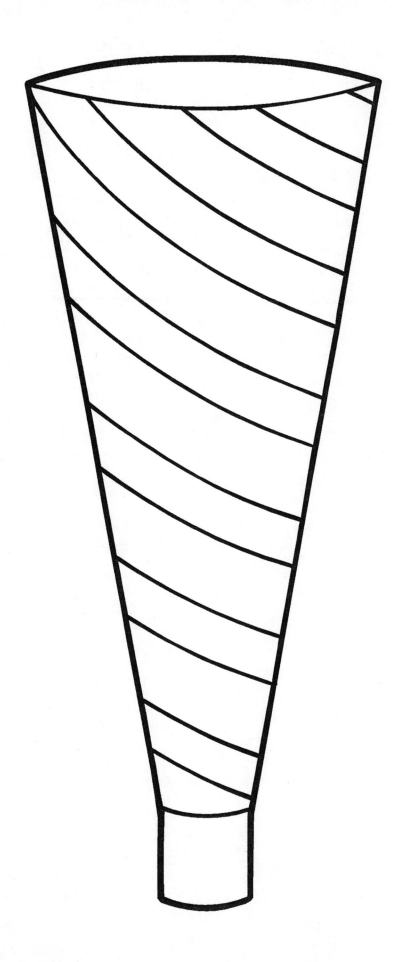

Party Horn   127

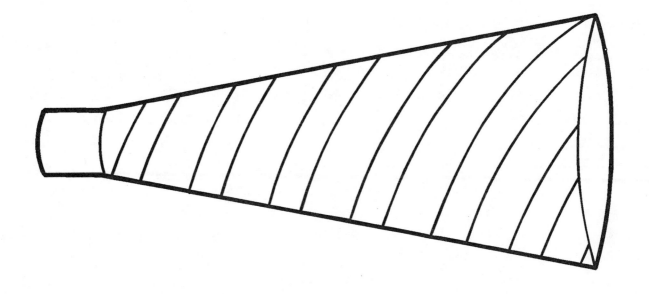

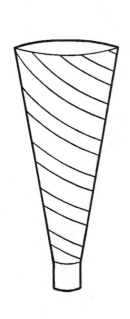

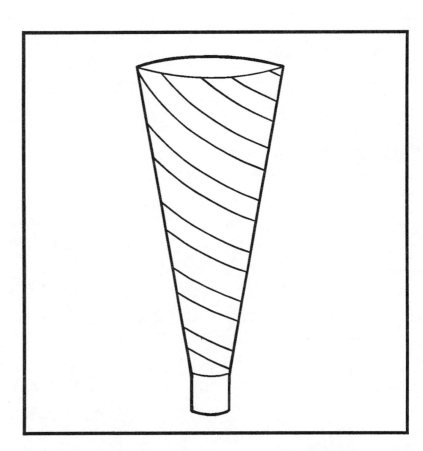

Party Horn 129

Chinese Lantern 131

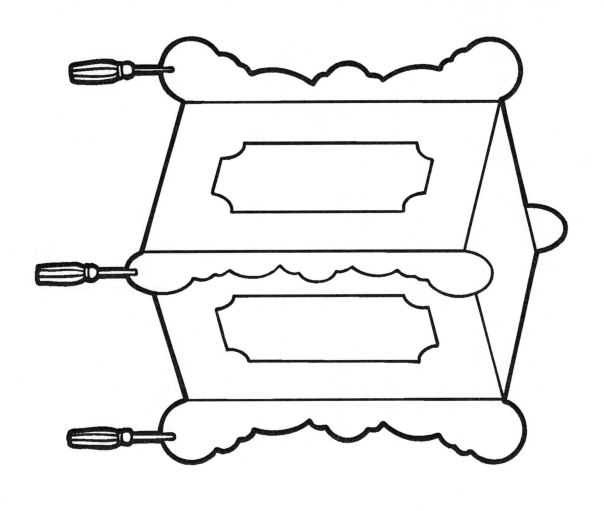

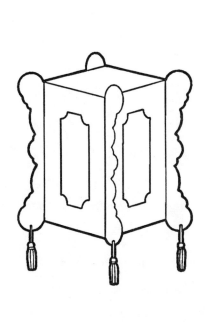

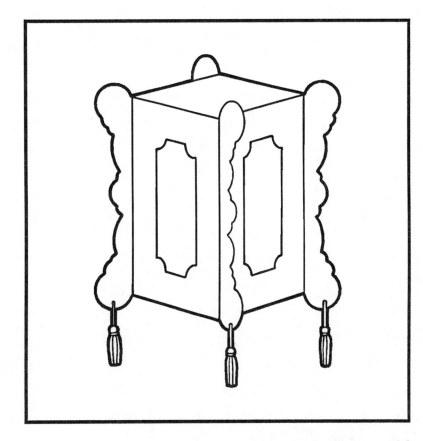

Chinese Lantern 133

Lion Mask 135

Lion Mask   137

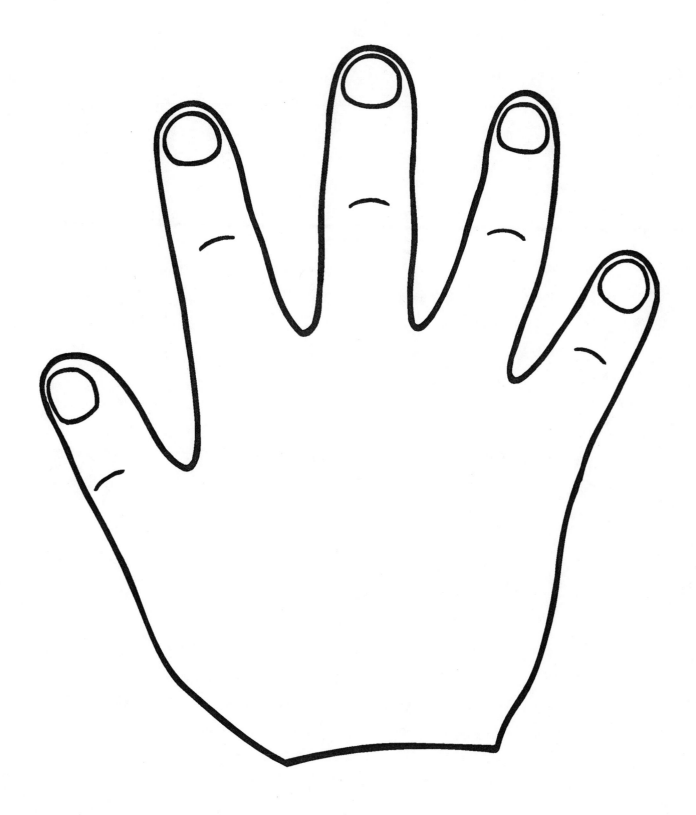

Hand 139

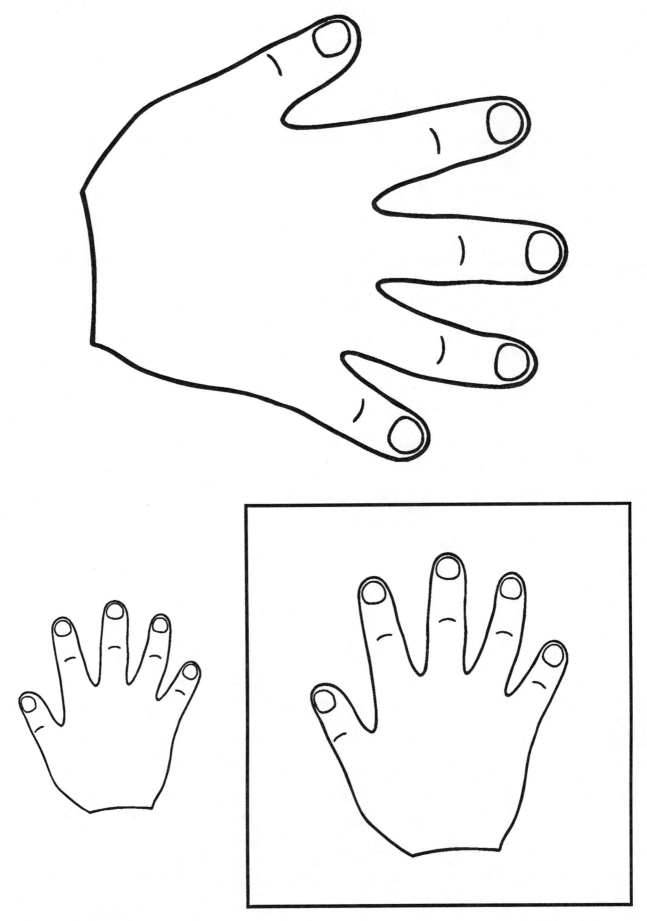

Hand 141

World   143

World 145

Lincoln Silhouette

Lincoln Silhouette 149

Log Cabin   151

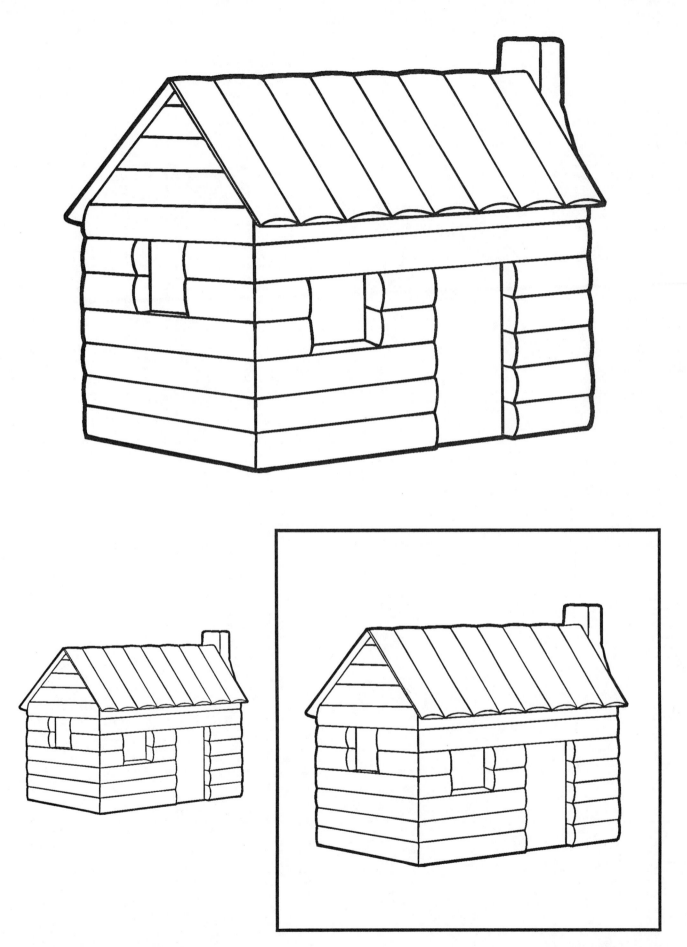

Log Cabin 153

Stovepipe Hat 155

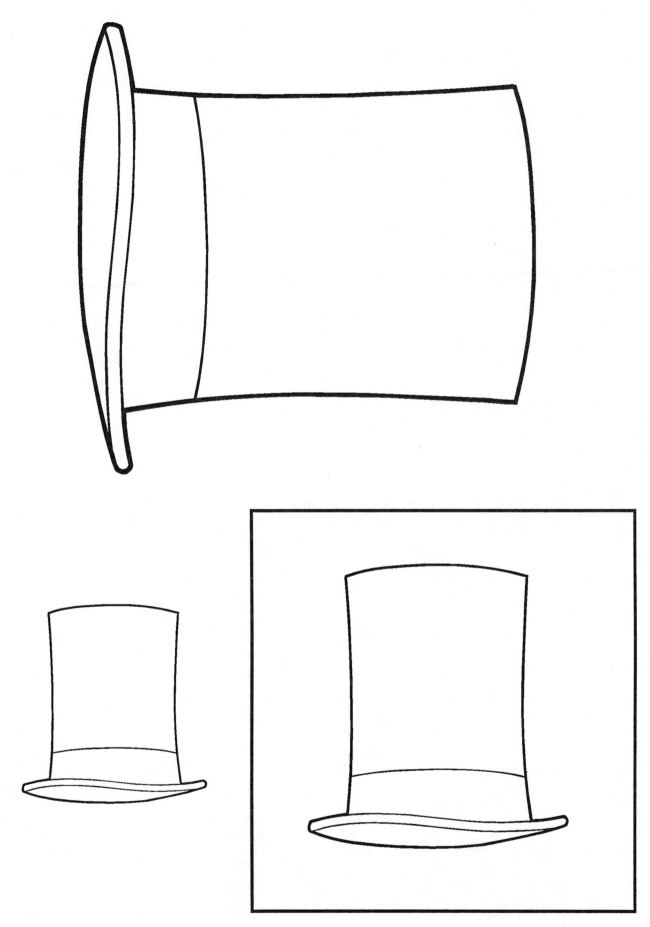

Stovepipe Hat   157

Cupid 159

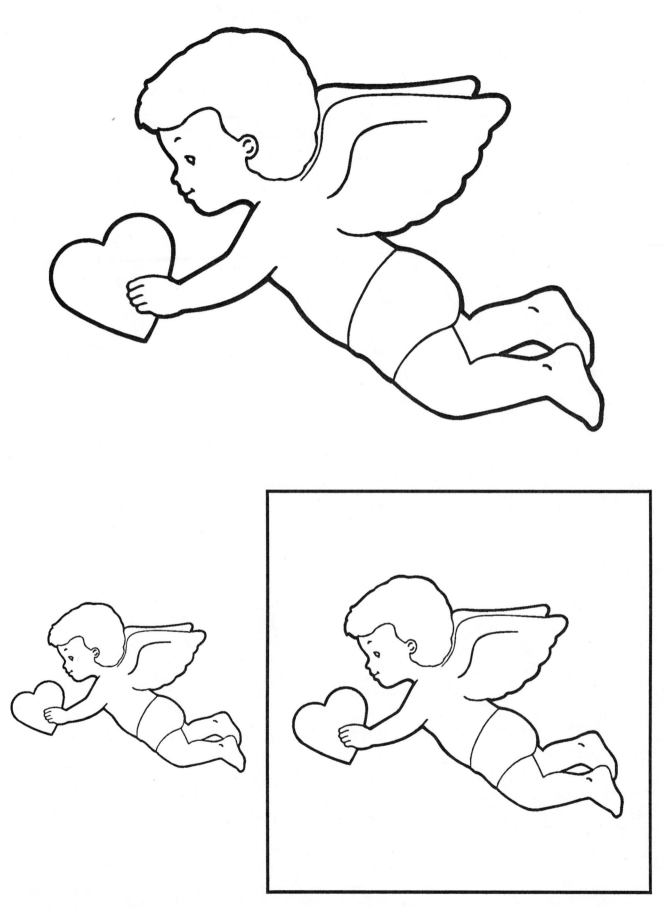

Heart 163

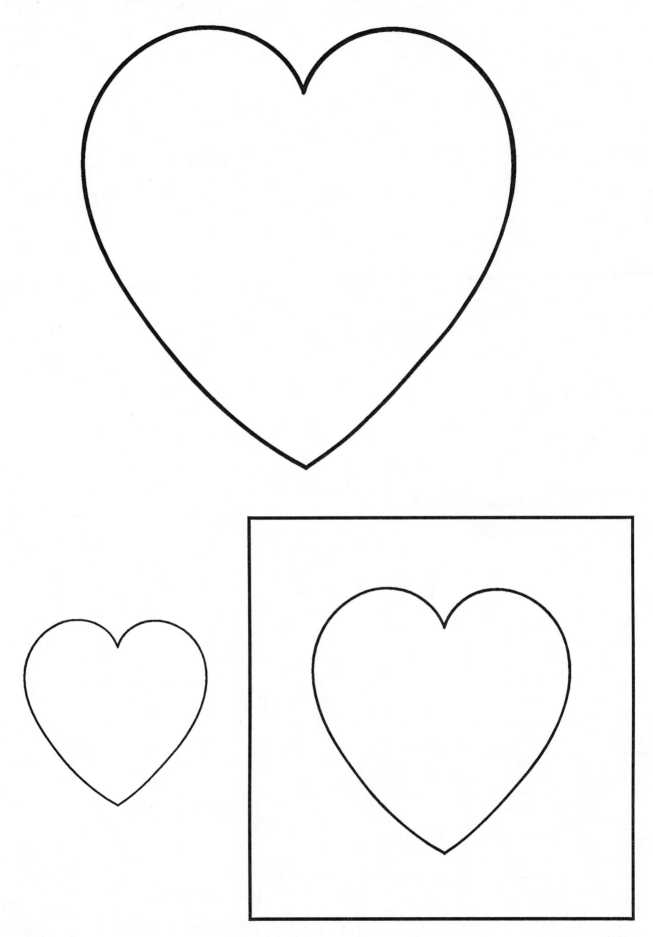

Heart   165

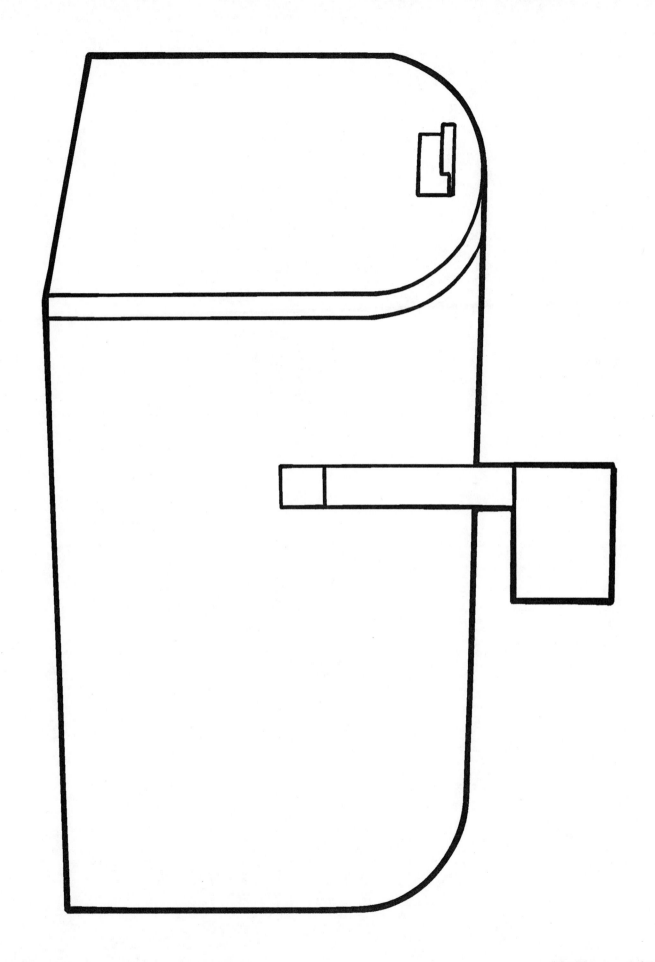

Mailbox 167

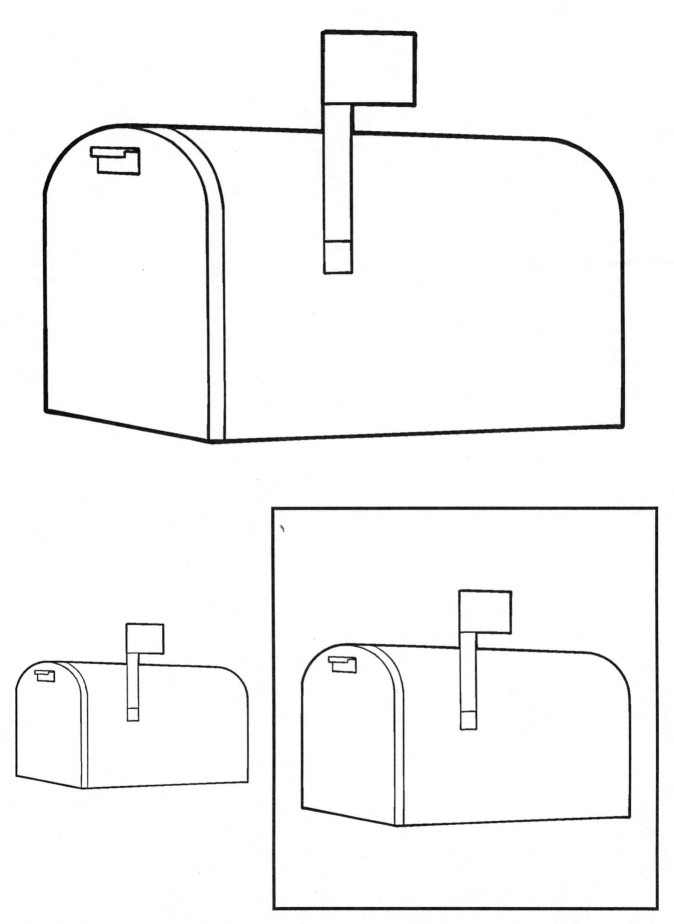

Mailbox 169

Be My Valentine

Cherry 175

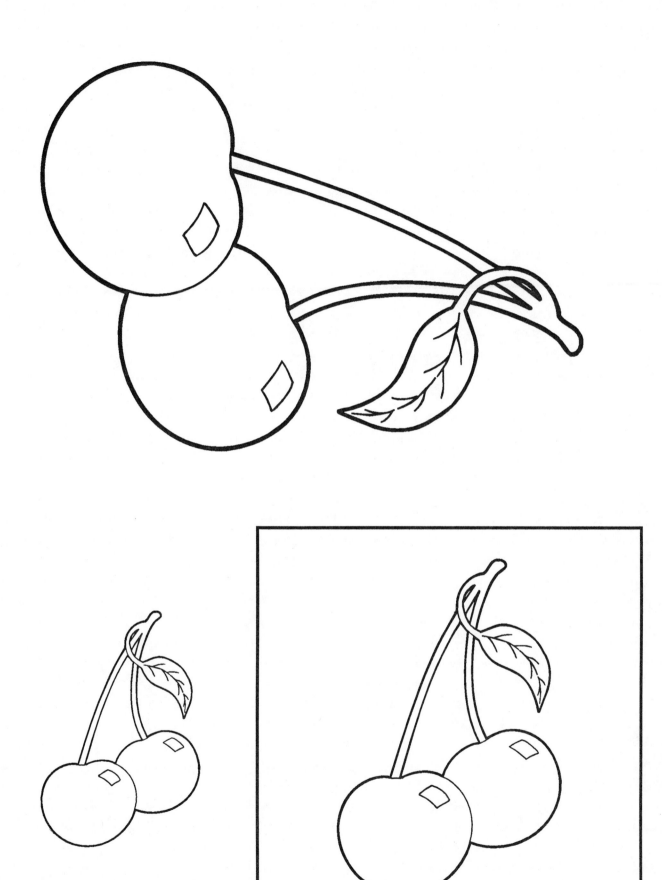

Cherry   177

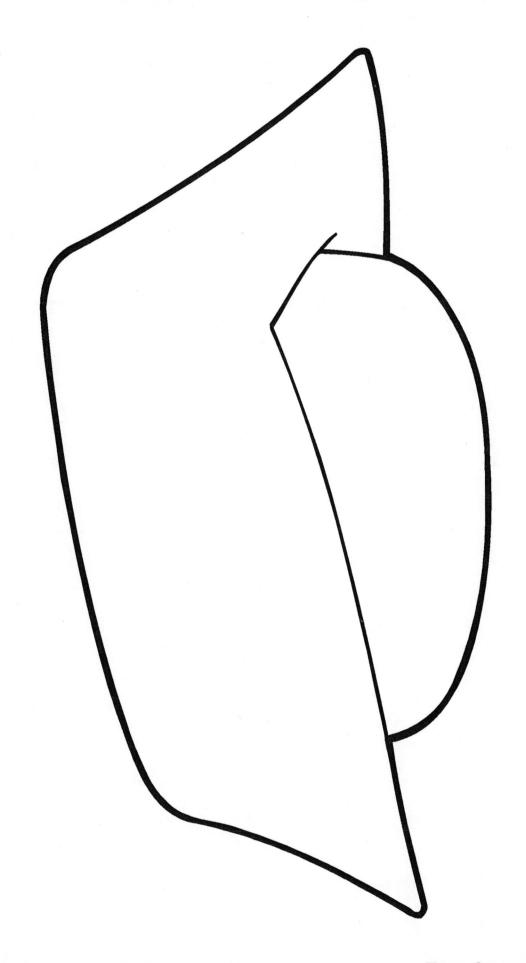

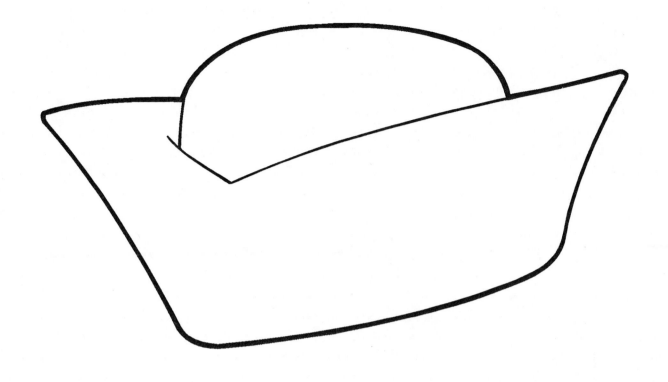

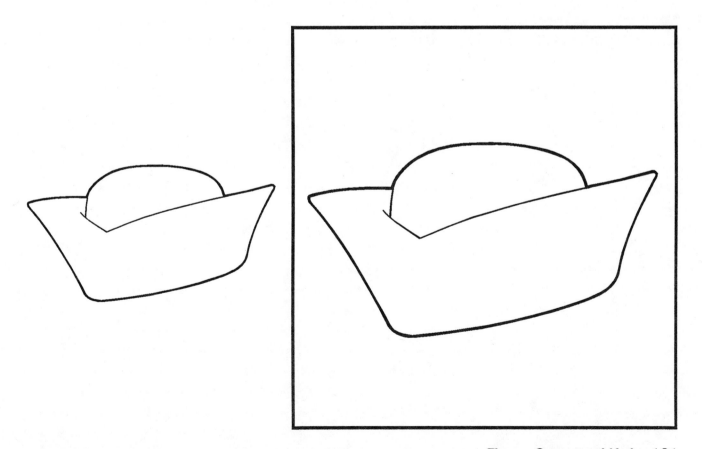

Three-Cornered Hat   181

Washington Silhouette 183

Leprechaun 187

Leprechaun 189

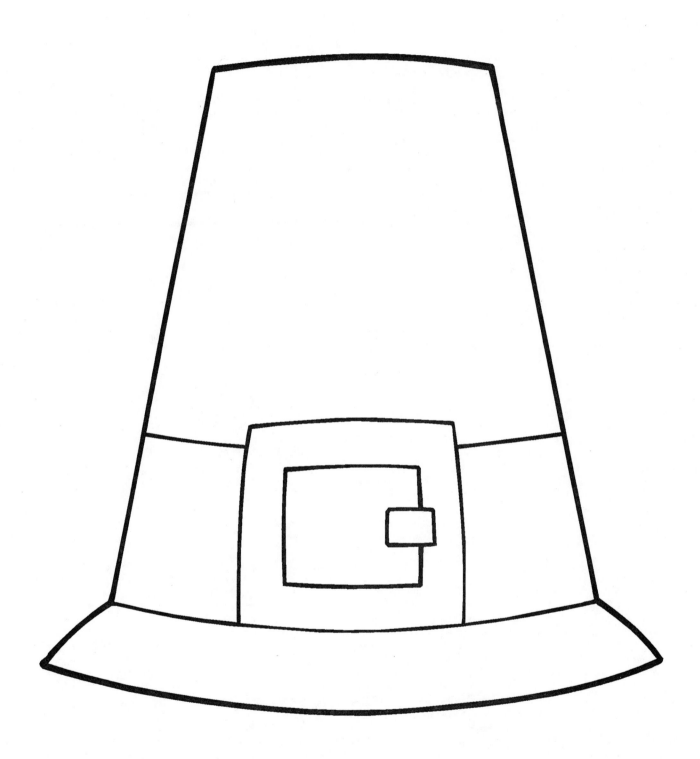

Leprechaun Hat 191

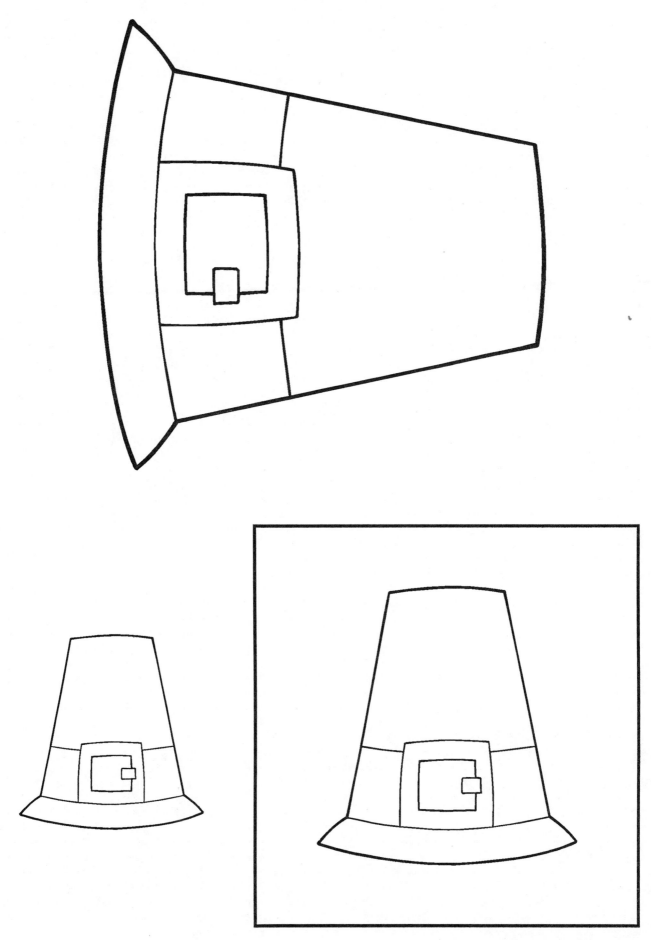

Leprechaun Hat 193

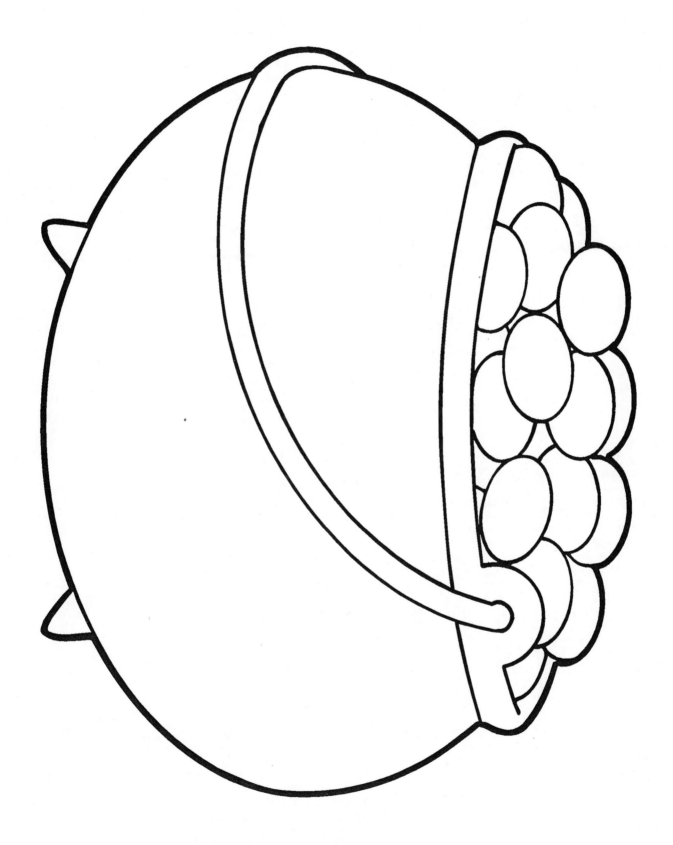

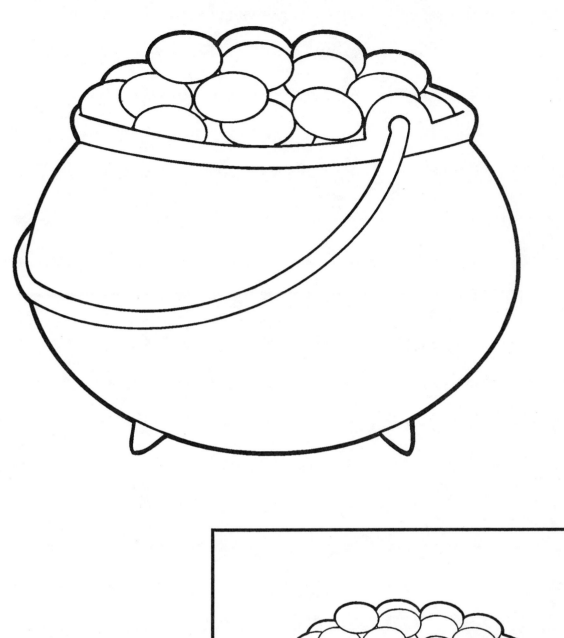

Shamrock 199

Shamrock 201

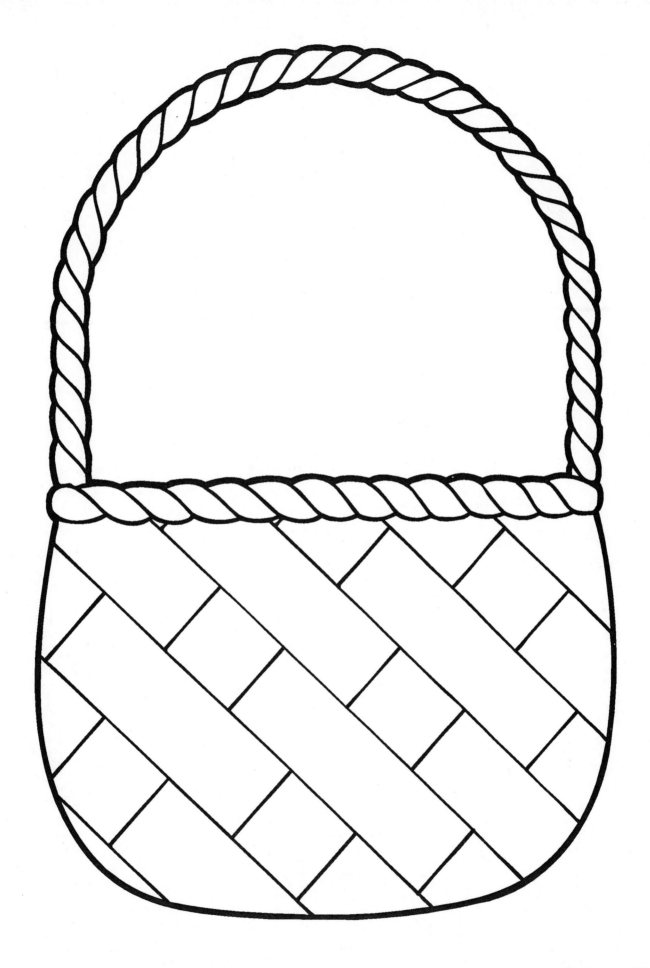

Basket 203

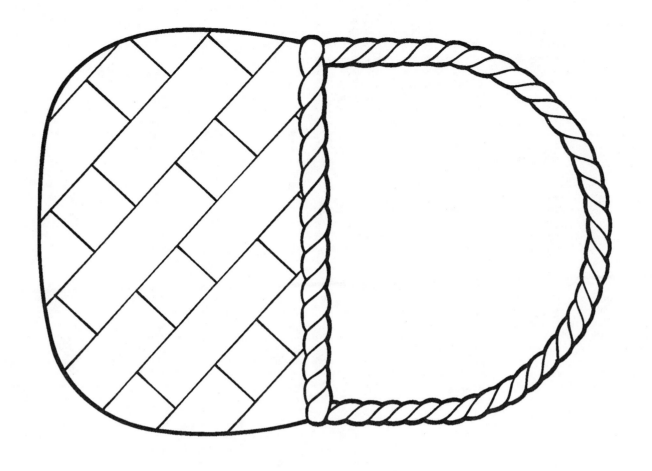

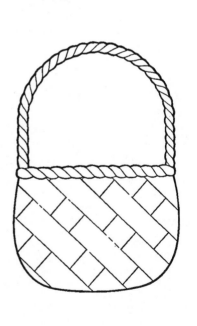

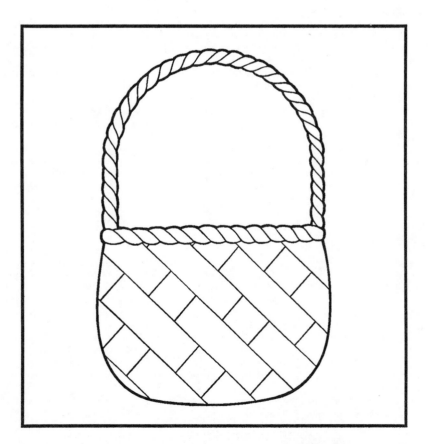

© Copyright 1991, Warren Publishing House, Inc.

Basket 205

Chick 207

Chick 209

Easter Bunny 211

Easter Egg 215

Easter Egg 217

Lily 219

Lily 221

Rabbit 223

Rabbit 225

American Flag 227

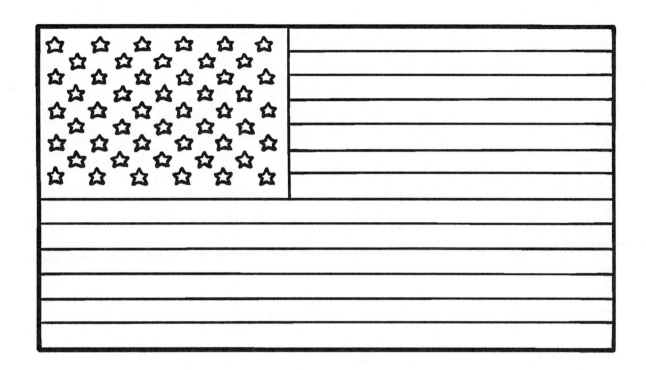

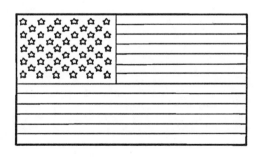

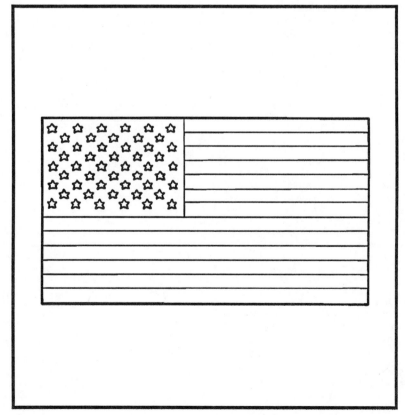

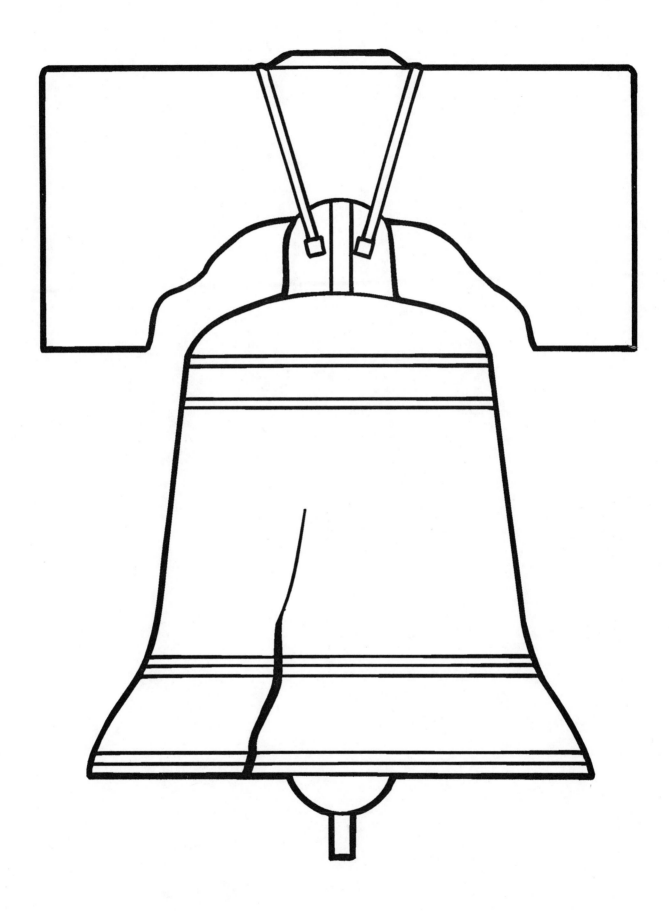

Liberty Bell 231

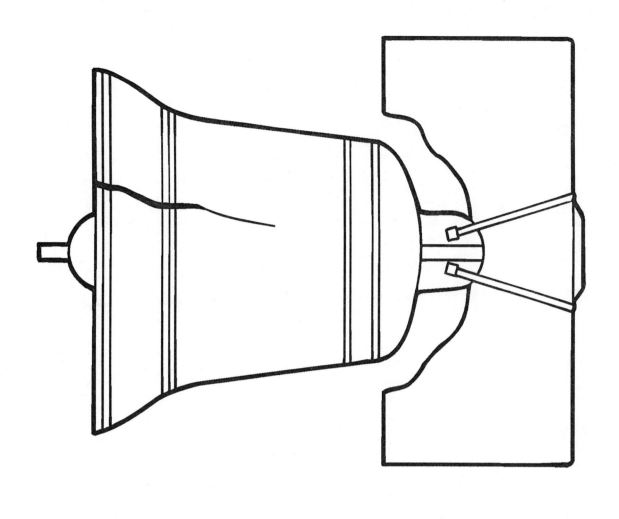

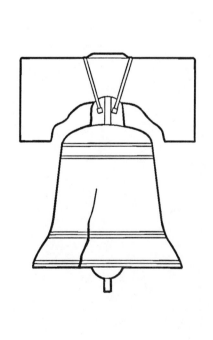

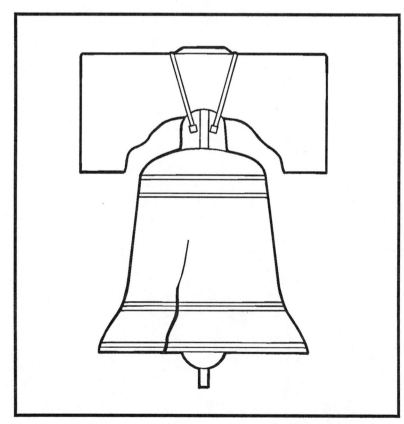

Liberty Bell 233

United States 235

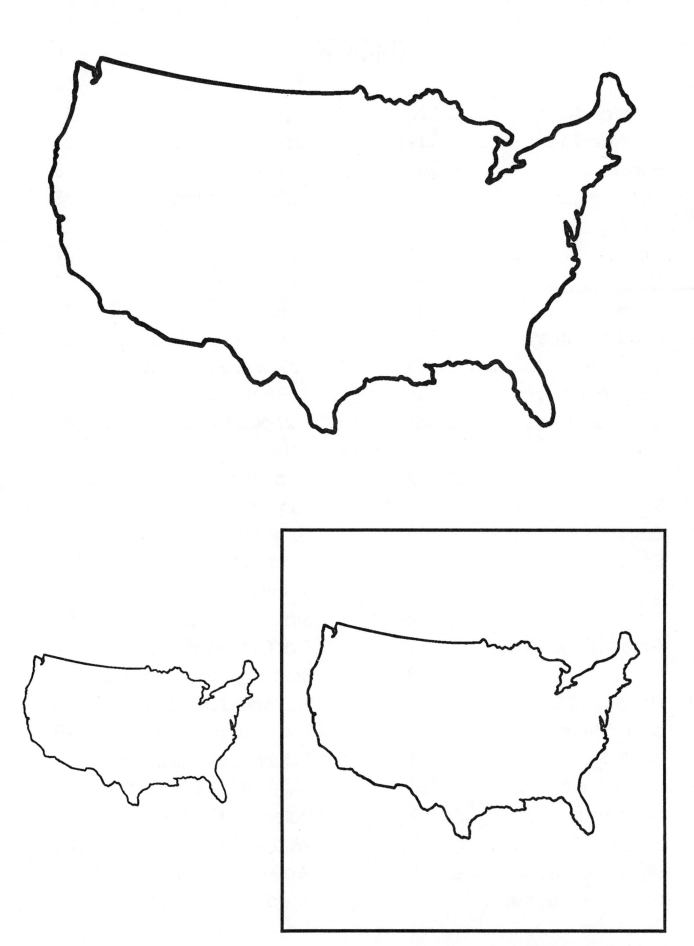

United States 237

INDEX

Totline.

Instant hands-on ideas for early childhood educators & parents!

This newsletter offers challenging and creative hands-on activities for ages 2 to 6. Each bimonthly issue includes • seasonal fun • learning games • open-ended art • music and movement • language activities • science fun • reproducible patterns and • reproducible parent-flyer pages. Every activity is designed to make maximum use of common, inexpensive materials.

Sample issue $2

*Individual and
Group Subscriptions Available*

Super Snack News

Nutritious food, facts and fun!

This monthly newsletter features four pages of healthy recipes, nutrition tips, and related songs and activities for young children. Also provided are portion guidelines for the CACFP government program. Sharing *Super Snack News* is a wonderful way to help promote quality childcare. A Reproducible Subscription allows you the right to make up to 200 copies.

Sample issue $1

*Individual and
Reproducible
Subscriptions Available*

TWO GREAT NEWSLETTERS

from the publisher of Totline books. Perfect for parents and teachers of young children. Get FRESH IDEAS. Keep up with what's new. Keep up with what's appropriate. Help your children feel good about themselves and their ability to learn, using the hands-on approach to active learning found in these two newsletters.

Warren Publishing House, Inc.
P.O. Box 2250, Dept. Z
Everett, WA 98203

TOTLINE BOOKS

Hands-on, creative teaching ideas for parents and teachers

Activity Books

BEAR HUGS® SERIES
Remembering the Rules
Staying in Line
Circle Time
Transition Times
Time Out
Saying Goodbye

BUSY BEES SERIES
Busy Bees–Fall

PIGGYBACK® SONGS SERIES
Piggyback Songs
More Piggyback Songs
Piggyback Songs for
  Infants and Toddlers
Piggyback Songs in
  Praise of God
Piggyback Songs in
  Praise of Jesus
Holiday Piggyback Songs
Animal Piggyback Songs
Piggyback Songs
  for School
Piggyback Songs to Sign

1•2•3 SERIES
1•2•3 Art
1•2•3 Games
1•2•3 Colors
1•2•3 Puppets
1•2•3 Murals
1•2•3 Books
1•2•3 Reading & Writing
1•2•3 Rhymes, Stories
  & Songs
1•2•3 Math
1•2•3 Science

MIX & MATCH PATTERNS
Animal Patterns
Everyday Patterns
Holiday Patterns
Nature Patterns

More books in this series!

CUT & TELL SERIES
Scissor Stories for Fall
Scissor Stories for Winter
Scissor Stories for Spring

TEACHING TALE SERIES
Teeny-Tiny Folktales
Short-Short Stories
Mini-Mini Musicals

TAKE-HOME SERIES
Alphabet & Number
  Rhymes
Color, Shape & Season
  Rhymes
Object Rhymes
Animal Rhymes

THEME-A-SAURUS® SERIES
Theme-A-Saurus
Theme-A-Saurus II
Toddler Theme-A-Saurus
Alphabet Theme-A-Saurus
Nursery Rhyme
  Theme-A-Saurus
Storytime
  Theme-A-Saurus

EXPLORING SERIES
Exploring Sand
Exploring Water
Exploring Wood

CELEBRATION SERIES
Small World Celebrations
Special Day Celebrations
Yankee Doodle
  Birthday Celebrations
Great Big Holiday
  Celebrations

LEARNING & CARING ABOUT
Our World
Our Selves
Our Town

1001 SERIES
1001 Teaching Props
1001 Teaching Tips
1001 Rhymes

ABC SERIES
ABC Space
ABC Farm
ABC Zoo
ABC Circus

PLAY & LEARN SERIES
Play & Learn
  with Magnets
Play & Learn with
  Rubber Stamps

SNACK SERIES
Super Snacks
Healthy Snacks
Teaching Snacks

OTHER
Celebrating Childhood
Home Activity Booklet
23 Hands-On Workshops
Cooperation Booklet

Cut & Tell Cutouts

NURSERY TALES
The Gingerbread Kid
Henny Penny
The Three Bears
The Three Billy Goats Gruff
Little Red Riding Hood
The Three Little Pigs

NUMBER RHYMES
Hickory, Dickory Dock
Humpty Dumpty
1, 2, Buckle My Shoe
Old Mother Hubbard
Rabbit, Rabbit,
  Carrot Eater
Twinkle, Twinkle
  Little Star

Children's Books

HUFF AND PUFF® SERIES
Huff and Puff's
  April Showers
Huff and Puff Around
  the World
Huff and Puff Go to School
Huff and Puff
  on Halloween
Huff and Puff
  on Thanksgiving
Huff and Puff's
  Foggy Christmas

NATURE SERIES
The Bear and
  the Mountain
Ellie the Evergreen
The Wishing Fish

Warren Publishing House, Inc.